MW01670973

The Smallness of Everything Else

by A.H. Lewis

Renee,
Thanks for the support! Here's to Allegheny connections ☺ hope you like the book!

Tell Maddi I said hi!

DORRANCE
PUBLISHING CO
EST. 1920
PITTSBURGH, PENNSYLVANIA 15238

Dorrance Publishing Co
585 Alpha Drive
Suite 103
Pittsburgh, PA 15238
Visit our website at *www.dorrancebookstore.com*

ISBN: 978-1-6442-6006-7
eISBN: 978-1-6442-6029-6

Foreword

Human beings are riddled with beautiful messes called emotions. Those who tried to live without them are called robots. Those who dove into them headfirst are called writers.

A single poem is not a constant state of mind. Each poem is a snapshot, a glimpse, into everyday life, with the fluidity and tumult of a waterfall. I observe, I study, I write, I rearrange. Some days, I'm the saddest poem in these pages; later those same days, I may be beaming like the sun I so often reference, because sometimes we forget that the universe can be found in our very atoms.

I have penned the emotions that threatened to implode me and swallow me whole, but the words that flowed, where the line lies between indulgence and catharsis, is where I chose to sit and swing my legs idly as if on a brick school wall. If you, reader, find that these poems help you to heal, to hope, to look to the future and revere the past, then I invite you to come, sit beside me on the wall. There is room for all of us.

No emotion is too big or too small to capture with words; no person is anything short of a whole poetry book themselves. Things like love, loss, tragedy, and triumph are just the terms of the human condition and no life is devoid of them, or any emotion, for that matter. Everyone has poetry inside of them. I just happened to write mine down.

If I hadn't loved writing so much, I may have become an astronomer to scientifically admire the heavens, rather than offer them poetry. But I didn't, so I offer the poetry to you too. Because in my experience, all problems, no matter their magnitude, can always be solved one of two ways:

By writing them down, or by looking up at the stars.

From my universe, to yours.

poetry

I write poems in my head as a means of thinking
and never even meant to before I realized
what I was doing
I thought I was just talking to myself
Nonsense, it may have been before, ramblings
Making comments in mumbles
Arranging words in chaos and calm
Asking questions with no response

It only became poetry
when I finally answered myself back

truth

They were the worst real words I've ever read.
Maybe because they were about me,
and you meant them to hurt, which is why
you never told me. About how the love had slipped
like oil through your fingers, if you could even
bring yourself to use that word. (You're no writer,
so it didn't sound that pretty either.)
Your web grew too many spindles, little spider,
we were getting too wound to keep straight,
so you kept a journal to organize all your lives,
all your thoughts like fraudulent diamonds,
in rushed sloppy writing in a neat little package
just for yourself: the gift of your own honesty.
Now it's my turn.

ascension

If I'm just a shadow, will you let me borrow some of your light?
Is it the substance I lack, or the darkness I wield?
Calling me a shadow is too romantic and sour.

What happened to me was far less placid.
I did not fade, I transformed.
It was more carnal and underground and molded in

wrought-iron hands, but what emerged was not what you sent away.
My eyes got darker and my mouth tastes like charcoal.
I leave burned handprints as a warning.

It was an ascension, painful and inward as a gunshot.
I am a shadow because you fear me. I can see the cracks
in your heart and hear the wind whistle through the pieces.

I am form and what happened to me is something irreversible.
Point your light this way and all that would remain
is my self, you think. Tricks of light, you'll be rid of me.

When you speak, we both know you are lying.
I was forged in fire like a blackened cauldron and I
have walked through flame without a singe and

fought my way back to the sky.
I am no longer anything but a god
and I have returned to demand my sacrifice in blood.

come one, come all

I start as the spectator full of wonder and magic
as I see the trapeze high above
knowing there's a safety net below them.
I clap for the tricks that are too good to be true.
And you, in the center of it all,
are the ringleader on your glorious stage.
The elephants wheel up on hind legs at your command;
the man swallows his sword of fire at your nod
while a woman leaps through the air
on nothing but a string.
I cheer louder than the crowd.

The entertainment comes at a price
when I peek behind the curtain between shows;
I slowly recognize the abuse it takes
to put on such a spectacle.
The discipline I thought you had
was nothing but a grand illusion
of mirrors and gasps.
The tent poles are made of fear
and everyone is limping.
The elephants are whipped with sticks.
And you are not the ringleader—you are a clown.

Those moments before I saw you,
the real you,
stripped of the image under the big top,
the mystery and enchantment
before the ruination of it all:

that's why we go to the circus.
That's why they call it
the greatest show on earth.

and still you stared

Expressionless you watched
with your head cocked slightly
I put the vial to my lips and tipped it down my throat
the poison cracked each rib as it passed
and dripped on my sunken stomach
it ate through my veins and drowned every pore
every breath rasping like drying cement
my skin glowed with death as neon does
my fingers went numb, my heart a fist of melted wax
tears wetted my cheeks as every cell burned
I collapsed to my knees and still you stared
I did not beg for help and you did not offer
the poison had been sweet I remember
your eyes met mine and you straightened your head
and as the last drop soaked into my nerves
my face hit the dirt and I drooled a goodbye
and you retrieved your vial from my cold dead hands

tectonic plates

The loss of anyone is extraordinarily hard when it is sudden. A car crash, a heart attack, a gunshot. The shock alone is enough to take our breath away, for us to blink a few times before we react. Before the pain hits. When someone is there one day, and the next they are not.

But I would argue that it is worse when you lose someone in a gradual way. When someone you love, over the course of many months, sometimes years, shifts as subtly as tectonic plates, you don't notice until the fatal earthquake. Because that loss is always fatal, when you notice one day, the person standing in front of you is a perfect stranger. And as you stare at that person you once knew, you feel how gradual and sudden the loss is all at once. The person you loved is gone.

The former, they didn't choose to leave. The latter, they chose not to say goodbye.

absolute zero

Change can be intimidating
to those who are unaccustomed
to it, which is strange because
life itself is change. Progress
is change. Growth is change.
It's the only constant we can
rely on because change
is inevitable in all aspects of
human nature across cultures,
languages, genders, nations, worlds.
Most people reject change, in fact,
because we have an inherent fear
of the unknown, the risks, the
unanswerable questions.
Do not fear change, but welcome it as you
would your favorite relative because it happens
whether or not you are there to greet it at the door.
I grew up in a place that sees all
four seasons every year, where change
is forced upon us every shift of the
temperatures, every phase of the moon
and cycle of nature's months.
We know that when the trees
shed their linings of leaves and everything
is bare and spindly, that's when nature is
getting ready for her rejuvenation.
We see it monthly, yearly, infinitely. We don't
panic when the sun's warmth stretches thin and
the leaves lose their color; we wait for

that first inhale of crisp autumn air,
bidding summer goodbye for the time being.
Winter takes over to put the world to sleep,
letting everything restart from absolute zero.
The stars above us rotate with time, so
why is a land covered in snow so notable?
A clean slate is how the flowers bloom
and the winds carry the scents of springtime.
They're all temporary by design, the seasons,
and I am grateful to have been a child raised by all of them.

finally

I look at you and see everything
written all over your face and the
way you hold your hands.
Mine too, as the scar slowly forms.
But when you look at me, you
appear as if you finally see
something dimensional. Something
to lay your eyes upon instead of
force your gaze towards. Something
to reach for, tenderly, and brush
with fingertips of caution. You see
a treasure, maybe, or a precious
jewel fit for a crown. I've been
waiting years for these eyes but it's too
soon to tell so be gentle for us both.
I may be fragile, but so is a bomb.

all I want

You are a constellation yet to be discovered
but I have named you in the meantime

I'll whisper it to you when you're ready
if you promise not to tell

The moon's craters are good for secrets
even as she blushes at my hand stretched to you

To see you is to love you; to know wonder;
to feel small and significant all at once

How silly am I to have claimed you
when all I want is to join you?

Horizon will consume the light as it always does
and I will welcome that darkness with pride

because only in the blackest of nights
do you, my love, command the whole sky

masks

Put your smile away, I don't want to look
at the teeth and eyes you show me
while the rest is covered.
You're fond of masks, you even collect them
and display them proudly like trophies
or severed heads on spears.
You make me wish I had one so you didn't know
what I was thinking all the time. Everyone
gets a mask but your Best Friend.
You make it seem easy and fun to hide things
like a game in a cemetery.
If a magic trick kills a few doves, the magician just
wipes off his gloves and reaches into the cage:
the dove thinks the cloak is freedom, after all.
I want to reach up and pull your mask off gently
to reveal whatever is underneath
and destroy it into nothing but dust
in my fingers. I won't waste this chance
to see you for real, so I won't stop until they're all gone and
I've memorized your face for the first and last time.

I loved you

I loved you but I had to stop
Your heart remained bereft
I gave you all I had to give
Until the day I left

save me

Shake me from this velvet nightmare, stir the tides of my blood. Wrap me in your arms and nestle against my cheek while I tell you about the monsters in my dreams. Listen while I tell you about the wretchedness of the demons that show up every night until I'm begging them on my knees to leave me be. Save me from it all, save me from telling you more, save me from telling you about the worst nightmares I have, where the only thing I need saving from is you—where you are the worst demon of them all.

battle scars

A heart
will bear claw marks
and bruised spots
where it absorbed punches
like quicksand,
but no apology
is necessary for this.
Swell your chest with pride
knowing that
you stand before us
with this heart of yours
and it beats
because you never
stopped fighting—
a war was won;
the casualties
strewn behind you are
reminders that you
were not among them.
You need not explain
the battle scars marring
the softest part in you,
for that means only one thing:
you will never want for
unearthly strength
because what beats
in your chest
is the heart of a warrior.

too old for lullabies

I've been handled in such a way
That has convinced me that I am hard to love
Too hard, in some cases
And I find myself with bloodshot eyes since
I'm too old for lullabies
I prayed to no one for it to be easier
Or that you were up to the challenge
I'm not a puzzle but a roadblock
A labyrinth of gritted teeth and clenched fists
Trying to fold a fitted shit and throwing it
In a balled mess in the corner
You're losing interest with every wrong word
I'm no longer the fun jigsaw but instead
The ramblings of a mad hatter

flood

When was the last time you cried?
I mean really cried, the kind that colors your cheeks
and strains your lungs and stings your upper lip.
The kind where you think you might drown because the
tears won't stop, and it's the best and worst state of being.
You can be sobbing or weeping, but silence is okay too.
    not everyone's emotions have sound
Your stomach is tight and that grip won't let go
no matter how many tissues you've sullied.

Your head is buried against your drawn knees—the darkness is
more welcoming than the   real world.
Everything hurts. Inside, outside, all of it.
It's all aching and throbbing with a panicked heartbeat.

When was the last time you cried like that?
Maybe you're due for it. Don't stop
until there's nothing left
and you're panting and empty.
There's a reason it's called a
flood.
And there will be more floods, more cloudy days,
more rain, more tears.

But there is always a tomorrow, and even
in the stormiest days, the sun is never really gone.
Release your flood and bring the sun again.
Wipe it all out, like God did, and start over.

convenient

I would drop everything
for the few people I love.
Conveniently, you were
the same way.
I didn't realize until later
that I wasn't one of those
few people to you,
I was one of the things
you'd drop.

the dragon

I am a fairytale with princesses
and knights in shining
armor and dragons.
But do not make me the princess.

I am the dragon.

I am covered in metallic scales and my
claws are bigger than your catapults.
I breathe flame and stretch my wings like sails,
but you'll never get close enough
to count the barbs on my back.
I sit in my castle in its isolated splendor
to sharpen my fangs and wait
for you to send your best warriors.

They think to conquer me for honor,
for pride, for glory.
They are all mistaken.
I flick my tail at their measly shields
and laugh at their fragility.
Send one, send ten,
send all that you have.

Send the one you call brave
and I will send him back a charred mess.
Send the one you call strong
and I will send him back maimed.
Send the one you call a hero
and I will not send him back.

The heroes think they have
the most to fight for.
The heroes are the knights
whose armor no longer shine and
whose swords are the biggest.
Send me your heroes and
you will not get them back—
I will use their swords
to pick their bones from my teeth.

all hail

Outside the lightning silhouettes
the fingers of branches
and the thunder rumbles like a ritual
in the belly of a drum.
The winds so fierce and the torrents relentless,
even the stars have taken to hiding.
Only Satan himself would use
such a storm to announce his arrival,
reaching out to drag me back
to hell on this lawless night.
But his fingers do not point in my direction
and his gaze is not on me.
He has come here for
you and your good intentions,
and the rains will not let up
until they have reclaimed their prince.

haunted

We always say that ghosts linger
because of their unfinished business,
but is that not the spirit of the living?
We ourselves are the shadows of ghost stories;
we are the business that aches incomplete.

a most extraordinary way

A phoenix from ashes does not rise, but teeters on unsteady legs in its dirty rebirth. It blinks its old new eyes and coos at meaningless time. It is no one, a creature that surely prays for death each time its core warms to start its next existence. It would need to die in a most extraordinary way: a being that cheats the reaper can't very well be blown out like a candle, can it? No, it would need to end like a firework of booming awe and vanish permanently in a cloud of smoke. What it would be, the phoenix dreams, to soar the skies as an angel instead of a bird. No wonder a phoenix is known for its tears, the ones that heal all but eternal life. A true curse it is, being immortal—being nothing, forever, but a pretty pile of ash.

last flight

There it is in my core, a palpable ache spreading across my limbs. It's not tears: tears I can handle. Tears I know what to do with. This is something worse creeping around inside me as it grows and gnaws and builds, the potential energy stored in my bones. There is a restlessness in sorrow, in sadness, in loss. An echo in emptiness. What is a human with a troubled mind and a broken heart? Is memory its own kind of death? Is it still grief when you're mourning the side of a person that no longer exists? Is it still grief when that person is you, or life itself? I imagine this is how Lucifer felt on his last flight as an angel in the clouds of heaven before his tragic fall into an eternity of hellfire. You used to be my wings—now I am ready for the flames.

the only difference

The only difference between
writing and bleeding is that blood
is a much easier mess to deal with.

everything but

If you listened to the sound of my heart
with everything but your ears,
you'd hear the tutting that doves make
when the sun glistens the dew
you'd hear the piano forte caressed to a melody
curtains stirred in a summer breeze
the bite of an apple that trickles juice down your chin
teeth clinking in a kiss like a champagne toast
the sigh at a cataract's edge before the plunge
the delicate murmurs of thunder
embers on all ten fingertips sparking to graze yours
and the stars exploding that made us who we are

Come closely and listen, for the sounds are all for you
relax in my arms and release that breath
take a minute, say nothing, think slowly
and if your heart should reply in the beautiful quiet
I will listen with everything but my ears
and hold you tighter in the crescendo of night

a wolf amongst sheep

When it's finally time to sleep
And I rest my tired head
I know I won't sleep easily
Because all my sheep are dead

They were slaughtered one by one
In the deepest realm of dreams
By the time I reached the groggy field
I heard the final screams

What killed them, you ask? A wolf,
Of course, that crept in like a curse
To maim and eat my little poor sheep
And probably something worse

Fluffs of white in puddles of red
Smeared the sticky grass
A massacre, a sea of carnage
A nightmare refusing to pass

The wolf was strong and the flock was gone
And I yelled through sobs of dread:
"Get out of my head and never come back—
I wish it was you that was dead."

The wolf turned slowly and spit out a hoof
As his face came into full view
And I gasped and cried at his bloody smile
Because the wolf looked just like you

home sweet home

The person you love
should feel like a home,
but people can feel like
other things, other places.
Do not force a person
into being your home
if they are not ready
for real estate;
do not make a home
out of a person
who sees you as a shed.
Tolerate the ones who are
a library, or a hospital,
or a sex shop, or a church.
Avoid the ones who
are a morgue.
But no matter what,
when you meet a person
who is a prison,
run in the other direction
and do not look back.

wasted

It shrivels my organs and blackens my blood to think of all your lies that made me smile, all your betrayal I cuddled to keep me warm, all your hatred for me simmering around your pupils. The energy I wasted on you could have rivaled the stars—and at one point, I would have given you those too. Had I looked more closely, I would have seen the snake lying in the grass waiting, not to strike, but to slither as if the reeds had never beheld a reptile. Cold-blooded and spineless.

bow & arrow

When you feel that someone
is holding you back, think of
yourself as an arrow and
they are the bow. And they
are not holding you back
so much as pulling you back,
back *back* *back*
until the strings cannot stretch any
further and the feathers on your
end sing to be released. You're waiting
to tell that finger to let go—no, don't
close your eyes, this is the best
part—because you know you're going to fly so far
that the bow becomes a speck behind you.
We're all just one second away from being
strung up and inhaling one last time to h u r t ling
through the air
towards where we'll land, to feel the tension
of the bow fall away as the wind
picks up around you like a kiss.
What you think is keeping you from greater
things is actually what ensures you
reach them—you'll more deeply appreciate
where you go when you see how far you've gone.
And while it's easy to see yourself
as just someone's arrow,
always keep in mind
you're also someone's bow.

a cactus

I swallowed a cactus
It's getting harder to hide
My mouth is full of blood
It's pricking my lungs
And my heart and my skin
Leaving holes where my smile should be
Finding comfort in my deepest shade
My fingers were the first to be claimed
By needles and quills and thirst
Or was it my eyes
Just gapes of Black in a moonless face
If I open my mouth the blood spills
But if I don't then I can't scream
When I breathe it scolds me
When I smile it cracks my lips
When I cry it blooms
Only the first line was a lie

proof

A mother's love is surely proof that heaven exists,
for there is nothing more pure and glowing in this world.
I have a mother with angel dust still in her hair
(she doesn't get it in the food)
that glitters in the sunlight when she laughs,
but sadly not all mothers love the way mine does.
Not everyone is so lucky.
Indeed, the way some mothers treat their babies
is sheer proof that hell is thriving.

the deepest part of the ocean

The aquarium is a great place to go
if you're looking for a dark mysterious
ambience with the beauty and
naturalistic wonder that is biology.
The way a fish has evolved to be its
own source of light, or the camouflage
of which an octopus is capable, or the
properties of a starfish that allow
it to regrow its limbs on command.
There's a calmness in the underwater realm,
in the tanks of floating jellyfish
undulating carelessly.
Everything is blue, the most relaxing color.
You can hear the bubbling of the exhibits
and the gentle hum of their filters.
The sharks swim mechanically
around their coral settings, roving the water
like zeppelins above a ball game.
The fish swim in huddles like mirages,
shifting course as one collective being.
Penguins waddle aimlessly, debating if they
want to take a swim today or tomorrow.
It reminds you of the deepest part of the ocean
where the universe was born,
right before the chaos of the bang.
Time ceases to exist in an aquarium
because you are encouraged to stare into these
watery habitats for as long as you are willing,
to appreciate their contents for the aesthetic

if not for the mesmerizing life inside.
There's nothing like being surrounded by water
to remind you of the very air in your lungs.

beastly

There is a famous tale—
as old as time,
if some are to be believed—
that proclaims that the way
to approach a beastly
gentleman is to give him
unconditional love,
especially if he traps you
in his company and his friends
warn you that he needs help,
and make him
your soul mate.
This isn't love,
unfortunately,
because anyone with an
uncontrollable temper and
a narcissistic temperament
would be your curse,
if you allowed yourself
to entertain the idea
of your inner beauty
bringing out the best
in a monstrous person.
(Be wary of anyone
whose prized possession
is a handheld mirror.)
He should be an adult,
a grown human being,
a functioning person

without a vase of dying roses.
Denial wafts off him
in pungent waves—
why should I,
of all people,
deign to fix my ways
for the sake
of the feelings of others?
Beware of the evil
around him too,
because it will certainly be there.
Whether it's the remnants
of childhood trauma
or an enchantress
that never left,
evil will lurk within him
even if the claws
are hidden for the evening
or he polished his ballroom
just so you could dance.
Do not do this to yourself.
Do not give up your beauty
to someone hellbent
on being a beast.
No one changes that much
in the name of

self-improvement;
it's not in an animal's nature
to apologize.

iron eyes

I was born during a cold war
(who's to say there weren't more?)
kicking and crying and naked
the same way I died, actually
Harsh and Bitter were my parents
and I teethed on spirits no one can pronounce
children of beasts birthed by ideology
run wild through these crooked streets
their screams would echo if the walls held their form
my kin are tameless with iron eyes
Winter will save us, She always does
we shredded the badges to burn the bridges
that lit the whole city in a glorious blaze
spare me the gin blossoms clutched to your breast
I'm plump with red revolution

algophobia

Monsters nowadays don't grab our ankles but grasp our thoughts
and don't so much lurk in the darkness as overcome it
The night no longer contains the blackest shadows
since we have absorbed them into our veins

Fear is the fall off the cliff when you're tripped
Doubt wilts your bouquet on your lover's doorstep
Death is just the bittersweet end
because pain is the scariest thing of all

Pain has no form but takes all forms
Pain is a paper cut on your knuckle that takes the whole arm
It's an ode of love from dead lips to closed ears
It's the presence or absence occupying your bed
Pain wipes the blood off its mouth with your piling apologies

Childhood is fearing ghosts and ghouls and goblins
Adulthood is preferring them
You grow up simply by realizing
that the monsters are everywhere
except under your bed

misery can't be bothered

Misery most certainly does not
love company because frankly
no one does except inmates
misery can't be bothered
to tidy up and put out a
nice spread and remind the company
to take off their shoes at the
front door and keep an expired smile
on her face while the company
overstays their welcome

no, I think

misery tolerates company at best
being miserable is exhausting much
less hosting a party for guests
misery prefers a quiet dark room
alone maybe with a blanket
and a warm cup of tea
the only sound her even exhales
as gentle reminders that
maybe company can visit another day
but not before her tea gets cold

who are you

I wish I had amnesia
the kind that would
wipe you from my mind and all
the bruises your memory carries
because you are tainted to me now
a corpse floating in the water reserve
maybe it'll be like an accident
and I will hit my figurative head
everything will be clear
for the first time and your
face would remind me of
no one and when I asked
"who are you?"
it wouldn't hurt me
and you'd know it was gone
I wish I had amnesia
so that when I looked at you
I couldn't even remember your name
so that when I looked at you
I could smile at you and mean it

height of the crest

The ebb and flow is constant, tenderly relentless.
The tide cannot resist but for the pull of the moon,
and even their affair strains the tendons of the shore.

Sometimes, with no wax or wane,
the light licks the water's edge like a lover in need;
a salty kiss at the height of the crest.

The heavenly body coaxes with ease:
the waves can knock you over,
but the ocean will swallow you whole.

the tricks of bandages

It's like a free fall
and your marrow becomes wind and your eyes are parched,
but down isn't a direction and up is a beating heart.
The hollow parts of your lungs where breath no longer hides:
the questions arise from there.
Did we jump? Was I pushed?
Midair, it matters little.
So many pretenses, now this one of flying.
How long is the fall? Where is the earth?
These are the tricks of bandages,
the sweet poison of empty philosophy
like a pacifier for newborn screams.
We have to be close, what else could there be?
Despite the view, it dawns:
we weren't meant to fly.
I dare to peek our progress—
there is no stitch of ground; we cast no shadow.
But my, how far we've fallen.

absence

The absence of you
would still be better
than the best you

that could ever exist

waves

There's a solace in the sound of
crashing waves and the smell of brine
that brings the center of your soul
to a stillness in the sand.
Let your inhales deepen, let your
exhales release what brought you to
the edge of the water in the first place.
Isn't it funny how sometimes a deserted
island is exactly what one needs?
The vastness of the sea in front of
you is welcoming, it reminds you of
the smallness of everything else.
The sting of words exchanged,
or the scald from the words
buried in your throat.
Relish in the quiet of precious solitude
and track your time merely by
the setting sun and the rising moon.
There is no rush on the coast,
the beach loves to entertain
wanderers in need of cheering up.
Pick up a seashell next to your toes and hurl
it towards the horizon—now do the same
with your gloom.
Don't drop your anchor here to stay,
cut its chain and leave it behind;
your sails are too full of wind to worry
if the natives are satisfied.
You've done all you can do, even if only

the palm trees sway in gratitude.
Enjoy your time while you have it,
whatever that means to you,
and allow yourself to be small
for as many moments as you need,
as long as it takes to return home.
Wipe the tears that fall
from the dynamic that tests you,
but refuse to let it wreck you.
You shouldn't have to bring
your own salt water to the beach,
that's what the ocean is for.

my choice

I could have stayed and made the best of it. But I chose to leave and make the best of myself.

the throne

I approach the throne of the devil
where he sits in waiting
as the fires of hell blaze around us.

"Move," I growl,

"you're in my seat."

surrender

The battlefield knows no mercy for foes equally seething, where there is no winner and no end in sight. Is it the forfeit you wanted, or the bloodshed? The victory, or my loss? Consider this my white flag of surrender, torn and shredded as it is. Now if you'll excuse me, I must tend to my dead.

your reflection

The mirror has never lied to you.
Where it reflects bright beautiful eyes,
you notice purpled skin of fatigue
and the sagging and wrinkles
around your cheeks and lips,
as if these aren't signs of a
life full of laughter.
Do you know how many
coffins will never see such faces?
You were created from the same matter
that shaped the stars and yet your
mutinous mind has convinced you otherwise.
But all mutinies must come to an end.
Look in that mirror again, at the miracle
of such a creation staring back at you.
No one overlooks the twinkling stardust
of your being—your limbs, your heart,
especially your mind—but you.
Be patient with your thoughts and give
them space to trust the reflection
that is trying to smile at you,
the one trying to tell you something.
Your body has been with you your whole life;
you owe it to yourself to love every curve,
every quirk, every guilty pleasure,
every claim of self,
for your body will be the
only place you ever truly live.
Silence all those slanderous insecurities

and listen, finally listen, to the words your body
has been telling you all along:
welcome home.

I want to be

I don't want to be your sun. I want to be your sunrise so that my stillness and quiet begin your day. I want to be your sunset so that you see all the beauty I'm capable of if you're daring enough to notice. I want to be your moon so that you may fully gaze at me in wonder with no need to shield your eyes. I want to be your stars so that I can illuminate your darkness like diamonds.

bit by bit

If you have a broken heart,
smear it with glittering stardust
to fill in the cracks and holes
like sloppy mortar between layers of brick.
No building, no structure, no foundation
can start with anything more
than the tiniest of pieces,
held together by the strongest elements.
Think of the most imposing skyscrapers,
the very tallest, even:
they all started as one single brick,
one drop of cement, one beam of steel.
Your heart may be shattered
and lying on the ground in shards,
but give it time.
Work on it bit by bit. Pace yourself.
These buildings weren't built overnight.
Someday you'll stand back and admire your heart
when it's finished and gleaming,
because it will be the center of your horizon
and the highlight of someone else's skyline.

flattened

You are a human headache and any time
you open your spoiled mouth all I hear
is a honking goose on a scratchy vinyl
I don't know how much longer
until your body revolts again
but this time
I hope it will be as merciless as you are
and my only regret
will be that I never told you face-to-face
how much, one time,
when I saw a flattened stray on the side of the road
I wished it had been you

self-exploration

I was looking for the hero but instead
I stumbled upon the lair of the villain

eulogy

"There's been an accident."

And just like that, the earth fell off
its axis and we collapsed from within.
Accident wasn't the right word for
what happened but in these moments
there are no right words.
There's a violent calmness to a noose
in a basement and other things that
no one should ever have to write or read,
that no mother should ever find.
It was all so unnatural, the order of things,
like walking into the ocean and hoping
to sprout gills. But instead, everyone still
needed air, our gasping just echoes adrift
in the chasm of loss.
I wonder if you second guessed it.
I wonder if it would have mattered.
Whether there was struggle or not,
the result was the same.
Guilt and tears cannot undo it,
no matter the abundance of each
or how much we're drowning in both.
But I will gladly help to shoulder
the burden you carried so long,
we all will, all of us who love you,
if it means you finally get to soar free
like a dove with wings of gold.

Because that's the thing about suicide:
regardless of what happens,
the suffering never ends.

the void

For what it's worth,
nothing is all bad or all good.

Life is not a dichotomy of this or that,
black and white, something that can be
neatly divided into two equal things.

So when I tell you that there is no love here anymore,
but there is also no hate, I mean it.
I neither love you nor hate you.
Instead, there is the absolute dead middle

on the spectrum of everything,
the spectrum we slid back and forth on for years,
where I will rest for the duration of your memory.
The void of the spectrum, where there is nothing.

No emotion, not even a flicker.
No giddiness or relief or contentment.
No pain, no sorrow, no lamentation.

Nothing.
Nothing at all.

macrocosm

I write in celestial terms because
everything is too big not to
Life love happiness sadness grief death
How can you talk about those things
as if they aren't each forces of nature?
As if they aren't gravity, but stronger?
They are devastation and purity
They are shaped by memory
and tragedy and promises
while you are the bridge of being
Instead of moving mountains,
you are the mountain that does not move
You are each force of nature and every natural disaster
You are the volcano bubbling to erupt
You are the rings of Saturn and the tails of comets
You pitch tornadoes and command the tides
You carved the craters into the moon and arranged the stars
You are a galaxy swirling the black matter with a spoon
You are all these things, and everything else
They bow to you because you are bigger still
You are the universe in its most exquisite form
and you were never meant to be anything less

stop

You tell me no and I write you poetry. You tell me stop and I reach out to hug you. You tell me maybe and I promise you yes. You remain silent and I tell you everything. You hide your heart and I let mine drip all over your shoes.

hungering

Poetry can be for anyone and if you disagree
you haven't found the right kind.
You don't get it, it's hard, you're picky, it's boring.
With that approach, no wonder you hate it.

If I could give you some guidance?

The best way to read poetry
is the way a snake eats its prey.
You open up wide,
until you think you might tear in half,

and swallow it whole.

Let it sit, let it digest.
It's still just a bulge.
You're probably uncomfortable and
overwhelmed with the weight of it.

That means you finally found the right kind.

Slither to a poem on your own
and indulge in its rawness.
Find the kind you're hungering for.
Never forget how good it felt

to find satiety through words.

mosaics

Despite everything, I don't want to hear you're doing unwell. I don't want to hear that you're struggling and not yourself. That people are worried about you. That maybe I should worry too, since I loved you once. My heart may be nothing more than millions of tiny splinters, but some of them still have your name smeared on them—probably always will, I'm afraid—and they ache to know you could be so much better than this. There's hardly a more difficult thing than acknowledging that you were the chains binding someone to their misery; it's another thing entirely to learn the chains are there regardless. I wish you could see yourself the way I did then, why I fought for you until I couldn't anymore. Something to keep in mind about my heart, though, and me, and you: we revere mosaics as pieces of art because broken things can still be beautiful.

my mother's garden

Do not under or over water the plants. Too much or too little will do them no good.

Water only the flowers that are thirsty. Dehydration and dead look very similar. Do not waste water on flowers that are dead.

Pluck the wilting leaves to save the plant, if you can. Save the ones that can be saved.

The soil in which they are planted makes all the difference.

No plant is irreplaceable. Arrange your flower beds, your gardens, your pots until everything has its place.

The seed is the plant. Do not plant seeds for tomatoes and hope for sunflowers to sprout instead.

Remove the weeds, roots and all, even if they look like flowers.

Every plant is different; every plant has its own needs. Tend to them for their wellbeing, not your convenience.

Watch for the ones with thorns.

Handle with care, handle with pride. They are yours.

Some plants are colorful. Some of them bear sustenance. Some are temperamental, some thrive on being left alone. But no matter what, they are all beautiful in the hands of a capable gardener.

aloft

In a world of floating and air
Heaviness and dirt
You are a tether, an anchor, a breeze
You are a mindful weightlessness
That holds me to a place of balance
You keep me aloft and I keep you from sinking
We are a hot air balloon in full flight
While others are squirming on the floor
Or bouncing around the clouds
We are right where we need to be, together,
Hovering just above the surface
As rocks that skip along a pond

your everything

I'm trying to be enough to be your all,
to be your everything,
but the ice in your eyes tells me I'm not,
the silence on your tongue whispers I can't be,
and sadness in your touch says
I used to be.

missing persons

There are a boy and a girl in my old pictures.
They are laughing and smiling
and hugging and kissing.
They look at one another like they alone
crafted the night sky just for themselves.

But then the pictures stop.
Where did they go?
What happens to a love like that?
Have they gone missing?
Did they die?

No, they didn't die. Their love did.

And it's not called going missing. It's called growing up.

anxiety

Anxiety is a paranoia that's hard to describe. The unknowns taunt you like ghouls dancing around a fire, prodding your skin with spears and making you nauseated and sweaty. The tunnel's light is dimming and the exit is shrinking as your thoughts rest on your shoulders like a vulture above a corpse. Anxiety has its own voice inside your head that you know better than your own. There's always a nagging thread of doubt you hold between your fingers so that if it unravels it was by your own hand.

That's how anxiety works. No matter what, it convinces you deep down it's your fault.

It's real, and it's all your fault.

moving on

You can whisper apologies to ghosts all you want,
but the thing about that is the ghost never answers.
When you accept your mistakes and finally move on,
you remember there are no such things as ghosts.

jagged on the edges

Think of it like tug-of-war
Only you don't know we're playing
But I'm sweating and my hands are flayed and the rope
is on fire and the mud has leeches and you—
You're just standing there
Looking back at me, doing nothing

I'm a film reel in frantic motion
Trying to find a place to play—trying to see a picture—until
smoke leaks out of my ears
Or it falls off its tracks in an exhausted collapse
I'm waiting for what's next
Watching, roving, fidgeting, lip nibbling
Conversations are never less than two layers:
The words you're saying, and everything you're not

The pieces of this puzzle are jagged on the edges
Covered in my bloody fingerprints like rust
Scattered on a wall with strings and pins
You're smiling—no, it's a smirk
Your eyes dart up and to the left—memory, not lie
Your hands are busy—no touching
Look, these pieces fit!—What do you mean
they don't? You can see—
No, that took me a long time, please don't—
Why are you mad—where is that piece—

The reel can only slow or quicken, the puzzle is impatient
Broken strings dangle from my wall

Pins wiggle loose and hit the ground like bullets
The smoke will combust someday
I haven't decided if I'll reach for the water or the match
(Which one would you hand me?)
A wordless shrug, one-shoulder, is the cocking of a gun
I don't know what the trigger is
Or if it's even loaded
Because when I do, it'll be too late
But I'll be standing there regardless
Looking back at you, doing nothing

note the note

The bloody footsteps are the hardest to ignore
My heart is racing but I can't turn around
I can't hear anything now except my own breathing and
The adrenaline alone will surely kill me, maybe the fear
I want no part of this so I have to run
Oh god, oh no—
He shouldn't have approached me
He left me no choice
Then all the blood
Is it his or mine? Oh god, definitely mine
The knife glinted, it knew where to strike
I thought I'd be safe to hide in the darkness but
The struggle didn't make a difference
I knew the exact moment of no return, it was too late
It wasn't supposed to happen, not like this
My last thought as the heart stopped: this is the worst way to die

This poem is two stories:
top to bottom, it is a murder victim.
bottom to top, it is the murderer.

appearances

The girl with the perfect body
has trust issues no exercise can exorcise.

The boy with the bright future
has a family that dims it every chance they get.

The woman you call CEO
works that hard because fertility issues are expensive.

The man with a beautiful wife and kids
cries in his closet because he can't figure out how to come out of it.

A glimpse, that's all you're seeing.
That's all anyone ever sees.

Anyone can lie with well-timed laughs
and just the right lighting.

Comparing yourself to others and wishing you had their life
assumes they're not looking at you and wishing the same thing.

Watch for the people whose smiles reach their eyes,
that's the happiness for which we all strive.

For someone else,
that person is you.

shrinking delight

The heaviness behind my eyes
gathers at the corners if I let it,
but today it stays where it is.
I am as small as a caterpillar
inching along a green stalk
with all dozens of grips
around the silky bridge.
I could bathe in a thimble
and find fullness from spilled crumbs.
No bigger than your thumb
or the buttons on your sweater
when I shrink like this.
It happens too often for my taste,
but down here next to the puddles of dew
there are pussy willows like skyscrapers
and dandelions like forgotten gods.
A butterfly flaps politely overhead.
Being small has nothing to do with my size,
as I sigh. It's my best kept secret,
tucked under the mushrooms.
I examine my fingernails too little to be seen
and bury them in the ground beneath me.
The dirt smells newer when I'm this close to it,
like I can absorb its nutrients through my palms,
discover the earth's age just from tiny handfuls.
The heaviness ebbs the filthier I get.
A slug oozing past lures a laugh out of me
that rings through hollow felled trees.
It's rained recently,

everything is soft and squishing
between my fingers and toes,
wet with friendly remorse, welcoming me
if I choose to stay small forever.
This time, I just might.

the first crack

I was expecting you to be perfect
when you thought I already was.
We may not have been meant to be,
but that doesn't mean we were meant to hurt.
It wasn't you at first. It was me.
It was preconceived notions.
It was what I expected
versus what I received.
I got the love I always wanted
in a different form,
and therefore I thought it was less.
If I had to pinpoint our demise,
I'd say that was the first crack
in the face of everything.
To say you lost our spark would be inaccurate—
I put it out in vehement stomps,
thinking I was saving us both from a fire.

it finds a home

In one of our school stories there was a woman
who was bitten by a rattlesnake and they
had to suck the poison out of the fang holes
it was already spreading as poison does
but they sucked and sucked and
promised her the venom would be removed
and everything would be better
she felt the poison leaving her body
they stroked her hair and everyone knew she would
be saved and live to see the happy ending
but for us there is always
the threat of venom
always more poison dripping
from fangs extended
just a drop is all it takes
it finds a home in the veins of its host
until it kills you or you become the snake
the only ones welcoming the poison are
those who were born with it all along

and the woman from the story?
She died.

pyre

There is a wrath boiling inside
like a brew of death in a charred cauldron
bubbling and spurting as it churns
fueling itself as it consumes all else
throw some more words in, those unspoken
are the most potent for the soul's rise
watch them sizzle in the wounds
next to the other scars:
the wrath has branded them
all as ours—his and mine—
and displays them to your empty eyes
give me all you've got and in return
you will get an eruption that humbles earthly spews
and silences the most vicious resistance you have
I hear nothing but a howl of relief in these veins
the rage consumes my bones, my tongue, my breath
it has left me capable of fury and flame anew
it's frightful, my indifference towards destruction
but I'm ready like you'll never be
and just when you think it's over and you're safe
know that there is never calmness
in the depths of my core
but a fire that burns slowly
to someday ignite what remains
like a pyre fit for a pharaoh

dirt

Your hair is the moonlight on the brow of a spotted fawn
chirping makes the leaves fall faster as
the stroke of paint dips once more
the wings flutter just for a second before
you whisper to me in river rapids
you smiled then, nicely for a summer boy,
in the valleys of the crested kiln
where I first met the freckles on the rocks without moss
we could have been something, you and I,
but waifs aren't meant to channel their lips into
something grander than a story
to pick me flowers is to hand me something dead
let's join them in the dirt and look up at the stars
as if six feet is enough to hold someone's lifetime

show me

Show me the colors of a sunset and I'll show you a sky full of stars.
Show me the rays of sun and I'll show you the shadows of the moon.
Show me your roving eyes and I'll show you my white teeth.
Show me your heart and I'll show you my heart.
Show me you love me and I'll show you I'll need it always.
Show me love and I'll show you life.

Show me you stopped loving me and I'll show you why it hurts.
Show me you don't care and I'll show you I never did.

metamorphosis

Look at you, broken and mangled and weak.
They ruined you.
They took your spine and crushed it beneath their
boots and stupidity and threw you
back to the wolves they raised themselves.
When I try to fix you, you run back to them. You return
to me missing a leg or with an ear dangling. You
flinch at my touch and snap at my pity.

"If you want to be loved, be lovable."

I tape your toes back on and sew your hair back to your scalp. I pet
your cheeks and read you stories. I rock you to sleep
while the rain streaks the windows. You smell like you again, your bones
are molding back together. Your skin softens under my lips.
Until Ovid's harpies call you back to the nest once more.
The line sunk in your throat tightens by the minute. Your back
is all smirking bruises and scars I can't kiss away.

"All human things hang on a slender thread,
the strongest fall with a sudden crash."

They've convinced you being broken is what
you need to be. You don't know the difference.
I hate them for what they've done to you.
I hate you for letting them.
You've been force-fed lies until you learned to swallow them
on your own, and when I try to pry them out of your mouth,
you bite me with those rotting teeth.

"Habits change into character."

You're exactly what they wanted—a ruined, irreparable mess.
We were both wrong. Those bruises were sprouts of wings:
the harpy you've always been.
I can no longer tell you apart, I have lost you to them entirely.
The nest shrieks and you take flight. I know you're not coming back.
You're not mine anymore.
Then again, you never were.

fairytales

When you are reading and watching your fairytales, little one, and sighing along with the hope of such a reality, do remember that no one is illustrating you. No one is writing your story, no one is writing your dialogue and setting you up to meet your soul mate in the woods. Your life is not predetermined by the magic of fantasy, the blessing of a happy ending. Don't expect to be perfect because you don't need to be. But do not for a second think you are anything less than the royals in those films, the monarch in the stories. In fact, be a good mix of all the characters: the heart of the princesses, the bravery of the princes, the loyalty of the sidekicks—and the conviction of the villains. Promise me when you grow up and seek these things in your adulthood, you will not let anyone take it away from you. Promise me that when they try, you will hold your chin high, straighten the crown atop your head, and bring the world to its knees.

gentle love

Please love me gently,
with warmth and featherlight kisses.
Love me the way the sun loves the moon,
the way the moon loves her stars.
Love me so that the bruises on my heart
finally fade and she can rest easy in your palm
without fear of being crushed in it.
Love me for all the reasons I am broken
and all the efforts I'm making to be whole again.
Love me gently, for I know what it's like
to be handled roughly by calloused hands
and a heart whose only job was to bleed.

womankind

What we do is magic
and yet you think to catch us and stop us
as if we could ever be tamed
but we simply throw you
in our crusted black pots
and cackle on the backs of broomsticks
our smiles are like black lace
that warn you we cannot be controlled,
a spell we have perfected for the fiercest of men
you tried to burn us once and for all
but how can you destroy something
with that which courses through its very veins

past tense

when did you close your arms to me and open them
to everyone else willing to look your way?
when did you decide that I was past tense?
when did we become silhouettes of ourselves?
when did you release me from your life like
a child loosing a balloon to the sky?

when was the first time you loved me?

when was the last.

when did you realize you loved me?

when did you realize you didn't.

the absence of things

Darkness and cold are not actually things,
but the absence of things. Darkness is the absence of light;
cold, of heat. (Scientists, I may have embellished.
Poets, humor the science.)

If something is dark, it is the amount of light
that is missing from a space. One says, “turn on
the light,” not “turn down the dark.” Darkness has
no measurement or unit on this planet.

Coldness is the heat being extracted from
another source. When you are cold, you are losing
your heat rather than gaining coldness.
Temperatures reflect heat and lack thereof.

So when you feel like the darkness is too much or you
feel too cold, remind yourself that what you should say,
instead, is that you need more light and more warmth.
In fact, most times a single object produces these two things.

The scientist may be thinking of the sun.
The poet may be thinking of a person.
A poetic scientist, or a scientific poet,
knows they are the same.

savior

I didn't need you to save me—you became the reason I needed to save myself.

tied for last

You keep me on your back burner
for people who forget you exist
I'm tied for last in a race I never entered
if there is a choice in your mind
between someone else and me
then there is no choice at all

mourning

The problem with always
trying to see the good
in people is that it operates
under the assumption
that people are acting
based on goodness
when in reality
what fuels them is
selfishness
hunger for power
greed insatiable
the human race has created
a world so vile that some people
wish to permanently
remove themselves from it
we should all be in mourning
for the species we could have been
instead of being the animals
we claim we are not
we are havoc incarnate
with the hollowest of snarls
and you wonder why
I'm always dressed
in nothing but black

might as well

We pluck each other's strings
the way only lovers do,
two puppets master over one another,
marionette sweethearts.
Lift my arms, I'll tug on your leg.
You raise my hand to your chest
as your eyes blink at me slowly
once, twice.
Your mouth opens and my mouth opens.
We know we shouldn't, I know you could
just as easily snip my strings and leave me
in a heap on the floor, and I you,
but we've tangled into deliciously intricate knots,
our X's from which we hang embrace
in their wooden hug.
Bring your strings over here just once more,
maybe a couple once mores,
before the real master comes back.
Just let it happen while the master isn't here.
It's too late to pretend we're only dolls
for the fun of it—we might as well move
like the strings aren't there at all.

just a warning

to those who don't know me
and for some who do

a writer is never at a loss for words

indeed we are inundated with them
there is no emotion we cannot articulate
no situation we cannot face

we pluck words like   wildflowers   out of meadows
and make a bouquet of phrases
fragrant verbs   stems of fragments
wrapped in doilies of punctuation

so when I respond to you
with silence

know this, and never forget it—

it's not because I don't know what to say

you are simply not worth the words

names

When you fling your names at me in
an attempt to insult me, it reveals
infinitely more about your own character
than it could ever indicate about mine.

If I am a queen,
you are a jester without a throne.
If I am a witch,
you are a mortal, weak and afraid.
If I am a princess,
you are a peasant with scraps for integrity.
If I am a shadow,
you are a speck of dust in a mausoleum.
If I am an idiot,
you are a caricature of your own potential.

Save your clumsy tongue
the trouble of coming up with more.
I've already laughed off the others
the way a lion finds humor in a gazelle.

in the name of fear

You may see how special
my love was someday,
how you'll never find anything
like it again in this world.
You'll realize it was
something to cherish,
something people spend
lifetimes looking for.
Whether it will be from
the way someone else loves you,
or the way you wish you loved yourself,
I'm not sure,
but when that day comes,
and you feel all that you lost
deep in your bones,
I hope you know what it took
for me to take it away.
What happened to make me regret
my kindness and patience.
I had to stop loving you
to start loving myself again,
and there is no devastation
quite like realizing
that love is finite.
You think I don't get it,
but on the contrary,
I understand all too well—the fear.
The fear of uncertainty.

The fear of change you don't want,
of love lost.
The fear of wanting to want.
The fear of more mistakes,
more failure.
The fear of time wasted, time ahead,
and the point of no return.
The fear of being wrong
about everything.
The fear of this,
forever.
It's a fear I understand
more than you'll ever know,
the fear that haunted me for so long
like a phantom of war.
Indefensible things done
in the name of fear
will leave ice shaped like me
in your veins
for the rest of your days,
but for the fear,
and the fear alone,
I forgive you.

trenches within

The earth is a mother too, you know,
and she bears beauty and blackness
just like you. There are some parts of
this planet, in fact, that have never seen
light, never felt the warmth of a summer
ray, and never will. They are the deepest,
quietest, darkest spaces you can imagine,
and yet, while they lurk below the surface,
the earth still orbits the sun as she always
has. She blooms the gentlest cherry blossoms
you'll ever see. She has a veil of constellations
and a burning core keeping her spinning, and
thunderstorms that remind you of the
irrepressible power nestled in those thick
clouds. She is capable of nurturing all her
points of light and her lowest depths,
and so are you.

It hurts, I know it does. And it might never
stop hurting. But if you need to retreat into
those cavernous trenches within you for the
peace and calm of nothingness, do so.
Ruminate; absorb the space into your
wounds; settle amongst the shadows.
Indulge in the darkness, but do not dwell in it.
And when you're ready for the surface once more,
look to the sky and rejoin us under the sun.

the beauty of tragedy

There are forces at play that we do not understand, as beings made of the very stars that surround us. When we experience the most harrowing of events, there is a transformation that takes place in the smallest parts of who we are until a new skin appears almost like an armor, a protection, against the potential of pain. It's something we all do, whether it's pushing our empathy away to finally catch our breath or scooping sympathy into our arms like an orphan. Humans are stronger than we give ourselves credit for, I think, and in the worst times, the darkest depths, the lowest lows, we forget our strength until we are tenderly reminded to take care of ourselves—that everything is temporary, including us. Learn from that which threatens to end you because you are not alone and you are still here. You haven't lost yourself, you've just lost your way, and that's okay because there is beauty in realness and healing wounds. Tragedy, sometimes, can be simply divine, if only you know how to harness it and march onward with the regality of someone whose life is more than their worst scars. Redefine the tragedy, but never let it redefine you.

words

Simply put, I write the words I need to read. At any given moment, I am a poem I have or have not written yet and I feel like I'll explode with all the words I haven't used. We flock to the well-written quotes of others because we think strangers know our own emotions better than we do, even though we are all capable of that buried articulation we so frequently crave. I am guilty of writing emotions that were not mine, but instead what I observed of the fragility of life in motion. All emotions are fleeting as they morph from one to another and we are ubiquitously all of them and none of them. Don't cower from the very thing within you that makes you human. Empathy is the backbone of poetry, and those who argue that are simply expressing that which they lack. Absorbing someone else's soul is half of empathy; understanding it is the other half. Poetry is that cohesion of the halves, the center of human immortality. There is no vulnerability like the rawness of someone's words, and I will gladly lend mine to anyone who needs them because no one understands that need better than the writer herself.

Acknowledgements

I'd like to thank the amazing, crazy, loud, fun, cackling people that I'm lucky enough to call my family. All my aunts, uncles, grandparents, and cousins, the ones who inspired some of the poems in this book. You have given me nothing short of endless support and love all my life, despite all the years of unending sarcasm I've put you through, and I hope I always make you proud. Not everyone is lucky enough to have an extended family that's as close as we are, and I'll never forget everyone's initial reaction when I told you the good news of having my first book published: "You write poetry?"

My parents, especially, have always encouraged me to pursue my passion of writing and reading, knowing that someday it would turn into something wonderful. You were right, like always, and I'll never be able to fully express how grateful I am to have been raised by two of the greatest people I've ever known. I couldn't have done this without you and know that all of my hard work is because of all of yours. You are the reason I started writing all those years ago, and you are the reason I'll never stop. This one is for you guys.

My brother, my absolute best friend and carbon copy of myself, can count on one hand how many books he's read in his lifetime and he still read my poetry without so much as a cringe. You were there for me when I couldn't even show up for myself, and saw me through the best and worst times that led to the words in these pages. You are the culmination of the good in people, the brightness to my darkness. If not for you, I probably wouldn't laugh at all. Thank you for supporting this book, tonty, and any that come after—wink, wink.

My friends became my backbone when I needed them most, and I'll always be thankful for all of you for being the recipients of both my real-life emotions and the ones I wrote down. Thank you for being the kind of friends I can trust with my deepest thoughts and feelings, and for reading them and loving them as much as you have. And for loving me as much as you have, too.

I couldn't have done any of this without every single one of you. You've all helped me in more ways than you know to become the person I am today, to have been able to accomplish this. I'm fortunate to be surrounded by only the best of the best.

Finally, thank you, all of you, for reading my book. Or being nice enough to pretend you did.

Index

CPSIA information can be obtained
at www.ICGtesting.com
Printed in the USA
BVHW041913031019
560165BV00008B/363/P

9 781644 260067